THE BIG I AM

by the same author

SIGMUND FREUD
I, LEONARDO
BETWEEN THE EYES
THE COMPLETE ALICE AND THE
HUNTING OF THE SNARK
(Lewis Carroll)

THE BIG I AM

JONATHAN CAPE THIRTY-TWO BEDFORD SQUARE LONDON

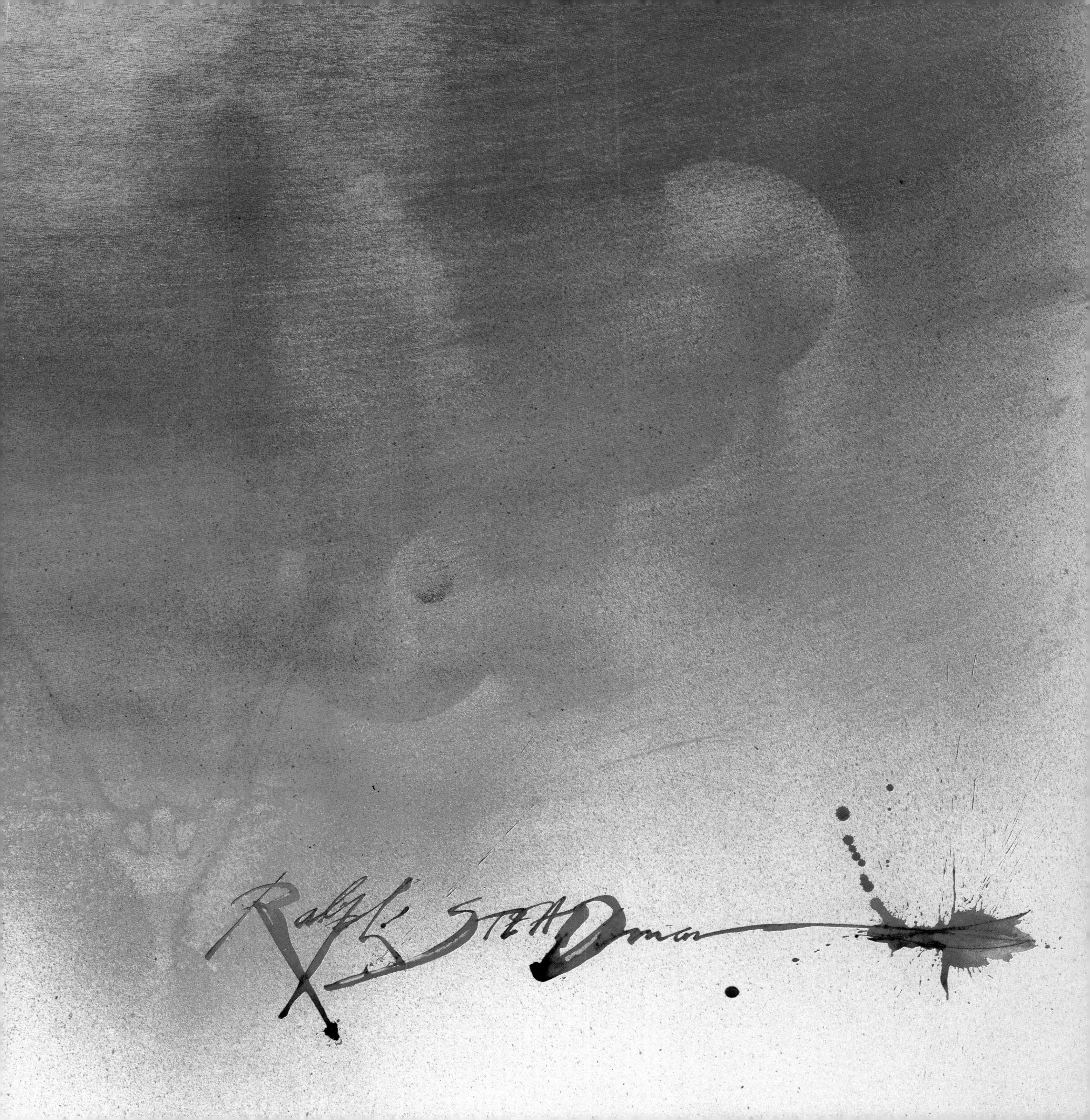
Ralph STEADman

Divine thanks to THE BIG IAN Craig, Designer of the Universe and false prophet who foresaw a failed deadline, but who still guided me through a wilderness of snakes and burning bushes to bring me at last to the promised land.

Blessings on John Farmer and Paul Bateman of STUDIO 24, 24 Redan Place, W2, whose photorealism brought forth visions of angels out of the darkest shadows of my pictures, and presented me on film with veritable stained glass windows.

Peace to Jill Sutcliffe, my Editor, who tempted from my words and His, a truer version of how it was.

Eternal happiness to Saint Thomas Maschler who never doubted, even when the way was stony and the writing was not on the wall.

Thunder and turmoil be visited in the pants of those who helped not when help was theirs to give.

Thanks be to GOD.

First published 1988
Copyright © 1988 by Ralph Steadman
Jonathan Cape Ltd, 32 Bedford Square, London WC1B 3EL

A CIP catalogue record for this book
is available from the British Library
ISBN 0 224 02471 X

Printed in Italy by
New Interlitho SpA, Milan

To those who would think otherwise

AND FOR PAMELA MANSON

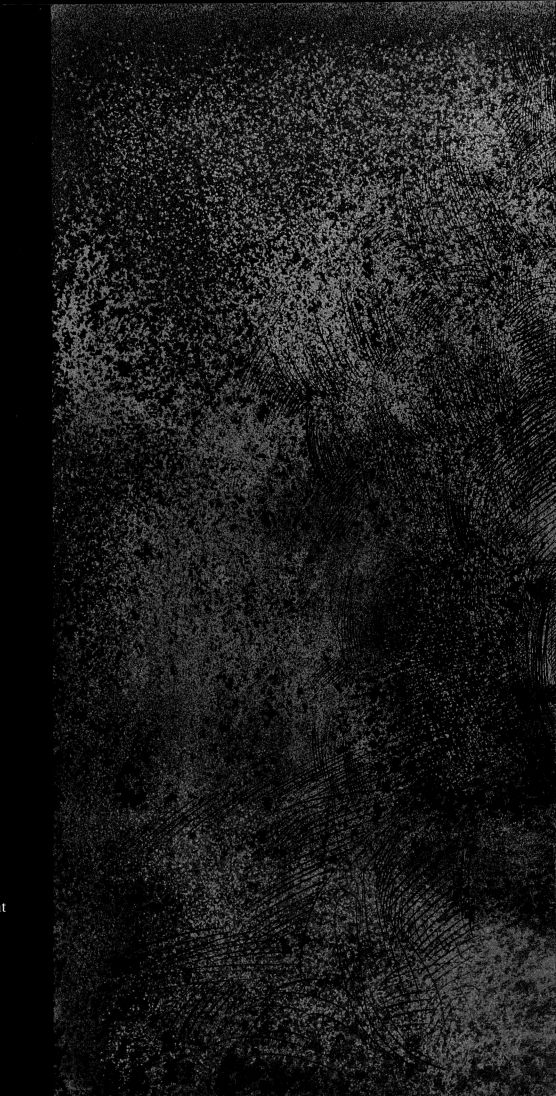

THE BIG I AM: An earlier beginning.
Arrogance and complaint from the original
bastard . . .

Before the beginning there was me; there was always me, but there
was someone else as well, but she, yes, she's dead.

Perfection — endless ecstasy — locked in a purgatorial embrace,
unable to escape. Condemned to an indestructible unity, for ever —
or so we thought then, my wife and I — for a long time anyway,
things were black and beautiful. We were even bored with it, the
blackness and our dark eternal ecstasy. We bitched and thrived in a
black void. No physical tangible evidence of our existence. Nothing
to see. Thought. Only thought was reality. Outside thought was
black. Inside thought was space and us, undulating. Nothing really
yet, except boredom. Blackness and boredom, unseen beauty. Why
change it? Craving, that's what changed it, the sense of
incompleteness; what was there to crave?

In that black perfection we were moving, oh so very slowly but we
were moving — imperceptibly at first. There was no specific moment
when we could have said, oh oh, we're on the move. That's not how
things began at all. There is no sudden changed state of being.
Things begin to move and they are not even moving, not at all. Just
— something different — a sensation you cannot even feel, at first,
but then, disconcertingly, a tremble, thunder down under between
us, nothing around us — ever, then.

THE BIG I AM: Retread of an earlier beginning.

Annotations for what seem to be a weird set of pictures with hidden depths that maybe only GOD knows and only HE will reveal, if HE wants to, that is, and which are open to any interpretation anyone wants to put on them. But don't try too hard. Why not relax and let His words pour over you like warm embrocation.

Before anything there was nothing, nothing but a blackness and a lonely tormented GOD, Whose wife had died in childbirth giving birth to the only live child they produce, and that child, EARTH, is passed over into GOD Who regurgitates it out of Himself and into the void, as a vomit. That's how close they had been. EARTH is a vomit, but it lives, and she dies. In His bitter loneliness GOD describes their love and unity, and the birth of the stars and the planets, all of which are born dead, a constant source of despair. The irony of His predicament fuels His resentful observations, and no one should presume to take His harsh dispassionate attitudes personally. Things are what they are and life is a vile and bloody struggle — but you know that already, so you are one step ahead . . .

Perhaps I should point out that the prose style, while lucid, has a tendency to erupt sporadically into some wild assertions and graphic opinions about us. At least I assume it is us He is referring to, though it could of course be another time and another place entirely, and who are we to ponder the possibility of that awful thought and further exacerbate the doubt? We are, it seems, if He means what He says, the pits, and we should remember that as we try to glean some guiding insight from His words. Gather comfort, however, from the fact that nowhere in this precious text He has so obviously been at pains to set down, do I detect the slightest hint that He is addressing you or me in particular.

There appear to be parts missing, or perhaps He abandoned those specific trains of thought, but we must, I suppose, be thankful that we have anything to go on at all.

We doubted our immortality because of it. Before then we had not thought of movement — or time. Time did not exist. Now it does — the moment we thought of our immortality. The inside grew bigger, yes actually grew inside us, swelled — we made it swell — we could have made it shrink if we had wanted to, but we moved with the new flow within us, a rhythmic flow and the space inside grew bigger. A flow and it seemed to live and grow and forge a life of its own. Not life — a will to move, that movement that doesn't move — but it's there, moving and silent. Deep inside that silence, that hollow that swelled, there was a cry that sent a shock wave through our thought and found its form in sound.

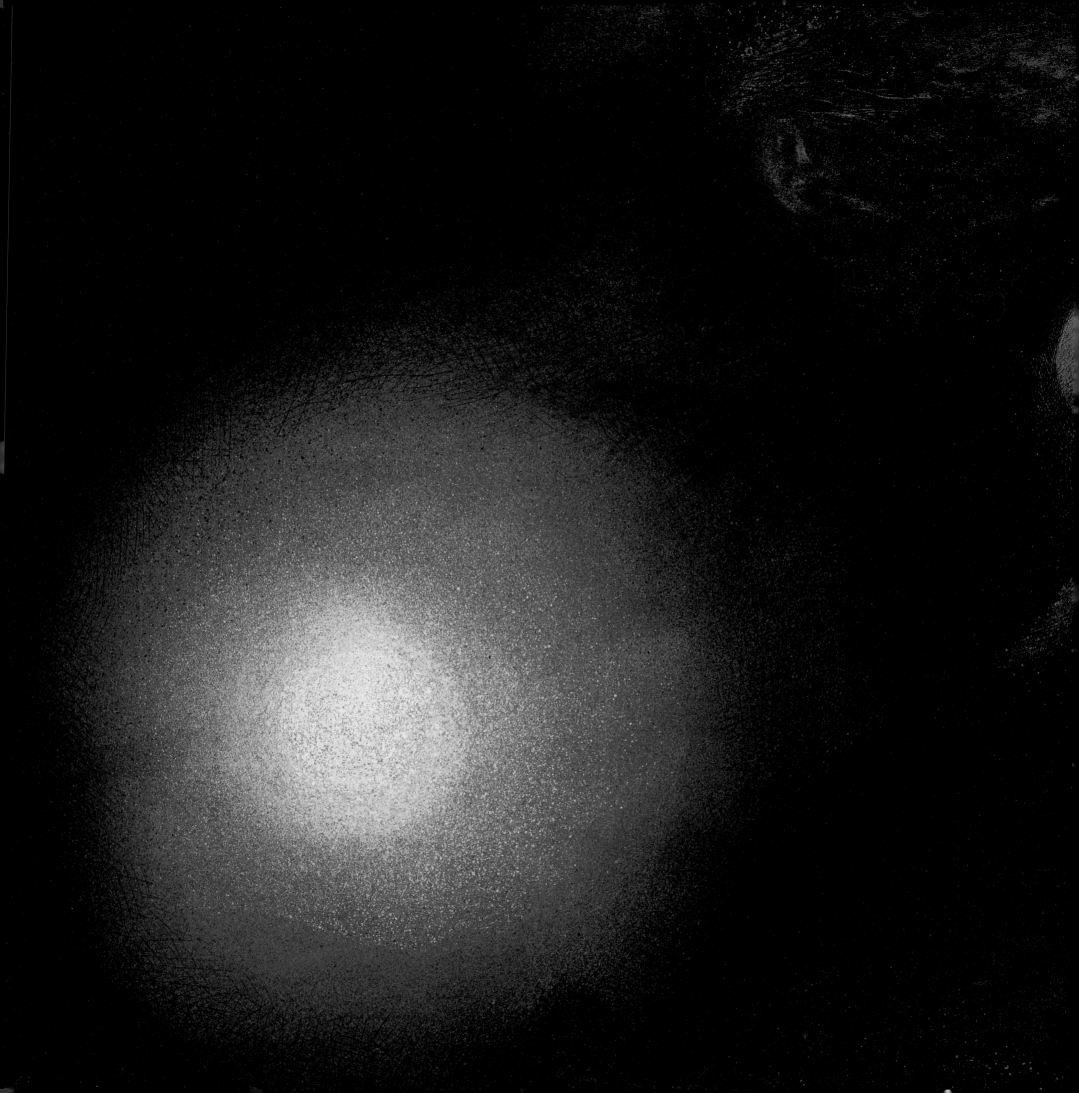

Until that moment, significant because of the sound, it was the first time, everything was the first time. We only, we specifically, had the first of everything.

The movement changed things. I knew it, we both did, and we tried instinctively to contain and stifle the intrusion. It gave form, something tangible to the space inside and we realised that what we had been was not what we were about to become. That slight movement finished it. And here we were, just beginning. That first intrusion — call it an intrusion — was a child, our child dead, stillborn, but it had nowhere to die. Well, it lived for a while, hardly time to curse its name. It had a name I don't remember, and I don't care because another followed and many others. A thousand million others. Their fate was still the same. The movement had begun: the not moving, imperceptible change. Spaces were filled and emptied into the blackness, unfilled blackness, never filled never changing change. A thousand million changes and for no good reason. A thousand million interruptions and then we rested, she rested, silence, the timelessness between ourselves. Our blackness seemed undisturbed but we knew. Around us tiny lifeless forms hung, and they moved, imperceptibly.

It was that inexorable movement, nothing was going to stop it. The vibrations of a thousand million experiences pierced our centre and the space was filled with another feeling. Call it sadness because that's what I call it. This sadness stirred our universe to crave again. Gone, the dark perfection. We imagined something not of blackness. What else was there? What could be not black?

The boredom drove the movement onwards towards something hot, something burned inside us and its heat scorched the boredom and the sadness. It burned and cried out; they had all cried out, but not burned and burning the inside of us to be outside. That movement again to change, away from what had been, nothing to stop any of it now. The burning wasn't the pain, though, that was to come. Now a piercing whiteness burst out of us, of her. She bore the effort, I took the strain. The piercing whiteness burst around us and we were naked before it.

Before the birth of the EARTH, the SUN is born to God and His wife and its brilliance, stillborn though life-giving, throws GOD into confusion as the startling glow burns its presence into the heavens and lights up the futility of their fertility, as it were, their acts of creation. There is no return to the previous black perfection and the SUN serves only to light up the evidence of their persistent failures. If it were me I would have called it a day long ago and found myself another hobby. Maybe that's why He is GOD and I am not.

Shock. A child emerged but such a child that one could wish it had been like the rest and left us to our black-filled sadness. It hung there, the opposite of all we had known, brilliant, throwing its startling glow into the void. It lit the inside of all our thoughts and drenched us in the shock of our existence. We had forged a whiteness out of black and yet knew nothing of its nature. I turned away to hide myself. The brightness was too great. Too piercing. We could see as though we had been blind and yet this brilliance threw a blanket over our thoughts. Our thought was blind. It was a mistake, I knew that, we both knew that. This bright new child lit up our universe. I turned again to look, I had to look: the once black perfection gone.

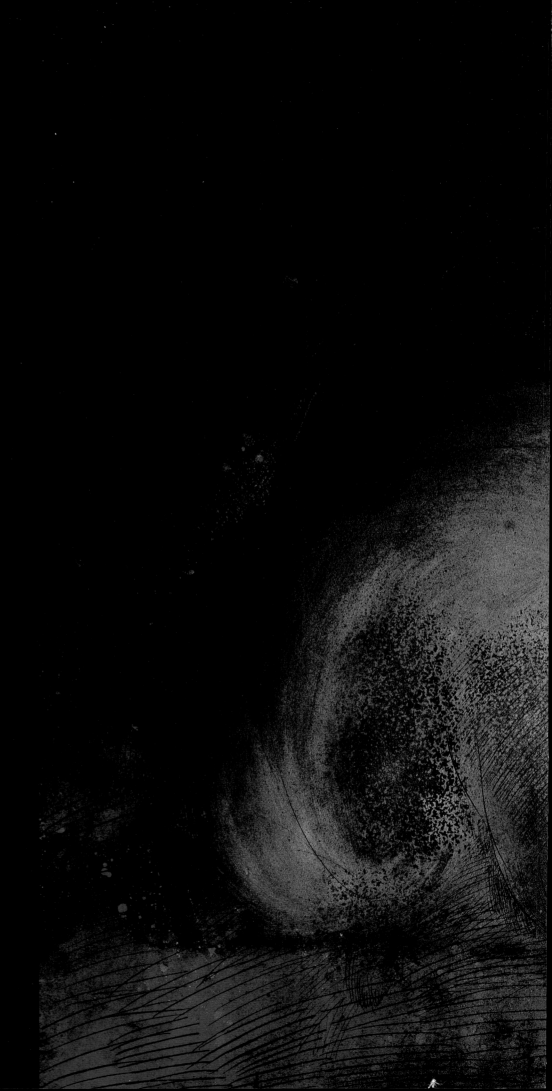

Yet another dead child is born to them and GOD hurls it towards the relentless light of the SUN in an act of total desperation. Instead of being consumed and destroyed in the intense heat, it becomes an orbiting satellite of the SUN and a relieving shadow for GOD and His wife for an all too brief period with each revolution.

In a million heavens of lost dead children, they trembled and shone. They will never know it. I can't bring them back, they are out of it, once created, never re-created, one turn each, it's only fair. Each one was now a celebration of its pitiful existence. Each one threw back the light of the new born child. Each was a vision of unwithering magic, deathless in death.

Now I was looking at her and realised with shock that my imagination was dead too. She was looking at me and I saw it in her nocturnal eyes. She knew, that was her strength and my weakness. I struggled to gather up the remaining darkness and cover my form for ever. An impossible task. This new bright child reached out to every corner of darkness revealing all in sharp relief. The process of decay had begun.

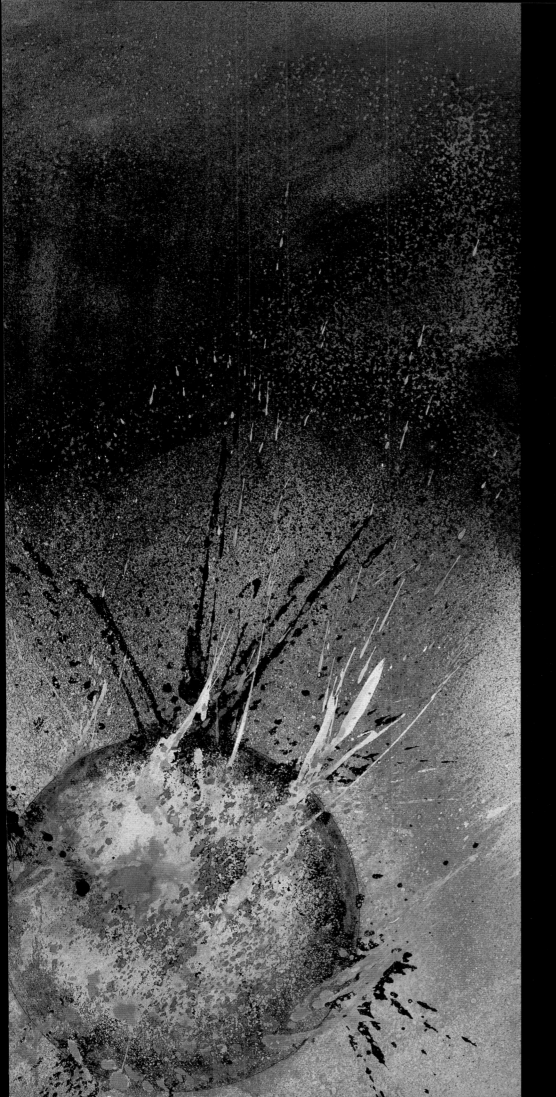

Each new child, though stillborn, has its own characteristics which act as placating charms to distraught parents. GOD's despair is near to breaking point and let's face it, He hasn't exactly had much luck. A lesser immortal would have given up aeons ago.

Time had taken over. It had been a huge mistake. No longer alone in total silence, an atrophy of perpetual calm, solitude and inertia. The absolute was violated and its tragic consequences were lit by this shining blindness. Its piercing light would not be dimmed. We turned inside ourselves again for relief more than anything, fumbling for something to replace our lost imagination. This new one tires me with its bright enthusiasm.

Then there it was, another child, another craving, unstoppable gurgitation. The bright one stood as sentinel, a constant scrutiny of my wretched form, our forms. I grew incensed and cursed its presence. It became a painful problem and deep within itself it knew and poured resentful incantations into the blackness it strove so fiercely and successfully to cancel out. Parts of itself became detached in great explosions, sending comets of light to greet its dead soulmates in the heavens. And the new child, stillborn yet again, I cast it towards the savage light of my despair. We thought the temperament within the bright one would pass over to the cold newcomer and its radiance would be dimmed. We were amazed. It was as though a friend had found a friend and, rather than burst out again in greater anger and burn it to the blacker heavens, it held this form to stay within a certain distance and revolve inside its warmest glow. Once in every revolution it passed between us and the bright one and we enjoyed the refuge of the shadow cast upon the heavens round about. This poor dead wretch was a blessing in disguise . . .

There were more children. One was cold, intensely cold, piercing with a sharp severity. Another came hot and red with rage, spinning into orbit around the others. There was one with colourful configurations surrounding itself with cascading circles of reflected light ringing through the universe, its patterns of divinity stealing a part of the bright one's light in some private act of defiance. All so different and alarming. One gave off fearful gases and the shock of a new sensation near overpowered us, a smell, unpleasant and foul. I banished that one to the outer perimeters of nowhere to be alone. I strove for order of a kind, cosmos, unlike perfection but a working solution for inevitable change. I had to allow imperfection but not chaos. We could not survive in chaos. All came out of nothing; well, out of our oneness, closeness. No one to blame but me, and her I suppose, our craving. No pity, there can be no pity for any of it, eternal movement. Remorse for ever. There is a reluctant harmony in it all and this, a floating deadness and a deathless brilliance to shame it all.

What happened next filled me with a thunder of
invented the inevitable but then I didn't realise it.
become a void. I am as they are, a succession of de
every unwilling effort stares back at me in blank re
escape from ourselves, to rediscover inertia, the bl
from a struggle, back to original blackness, the wor
— eternal ecstasy. No way back! Then incomplete
craving to fill the space again, just once more.

This time would be different. This time untouc
chasms darker than we ever knew were swelling ou
pushing for release. A relentless selfwilled force of
forward. This time a pulsing throbbing interior, pa
of its restraining, gentle but restraining prison of n
held it, held it back waiting for a moment, the righ
bursting walls of well-filled space struggling. Ther
restraint, but she tried. The love of trying, trying to
sensation, a pulling away to an outside. And me, th
were in this together, our space in turmoil and a no
tragic end to a new beginning. That moment I live
passing over a struggling terrible energy, her love i
into me, shuddered into me, me!

My love was gone. I was alone with this — this t
mindless of me and consumed by its own desire to
would be free, but I held back, repressing its birth
defiance. Internal pressure mounted and rose abov
resistance. It became a nauseous power. I retched
trying to deny the inevitable explosion. I sank bene
a rising tide, vomiting all out into an uncaring void

A hissing wind rushed through the corridors of my senses as my inner being disgorged itself, leaving behind a frame of cosmic tissues, finding relief only in a state as near death as death itself. All was spent and I was close to blackness again.

*GOD falls into a coma and dreams after His exertions and Her death
throes, inventing the devil as part of Himself and a safety valve to release
His fury in times of stress. To be able to blame someone else for one's own
mistakes and inadequacies is such a reassuring pastime. But this devil
doesn't seem to play a major role in the overall scheme of things, since GOD
Himself appears to have absolutely no moral sense whatsoever. We have
invented that and along with it our own guilt-provoking versions. The idea
that GOD invented the devil to tempt us is highly subjective anyway. The
temptation is to credit Him with far more intelligence than He actually has,
since our appearance, as you will see, is a complete surprise to Him.*

I dreamed I was not alone. I was floating and enjoying the act of
creation. I dreamed I was being admired, envied and even glorified
for miraculous work. I was at the height of my powers and all around
glowed with the radiance of my work. And I was not alone. Envy sat
at my right hand with absolutely nothing to do and nothing to be
proud of. That could have been me but I was the dreamer and this
creature beside me is full of doubt. It is so full of doubt because it
knows only that at some time I will awake from my dream and this
wretched figment of my imagination will be gone and maybe gone for
ever. I may never conjure up its presence again, for I would only do
so to heap upon it the blame for my own mistakes. But in my dream I
have made no mistakes and therefore there is no need for blame.
There is, of course, fear and despair, *its* fear and despair, and its
envy, knowing what I have created and knowing its own fate. Its fate:
that it exists only because I thought it into existence. Its doubt is its
certainty of sometime and its torment can be the uncertainty of
when. When I wake up.
   Since this is *my* dream I will be the happy one and burden the
creature with all the torment that drove me to this place of refuge. It
is only a game of course, relief from all my disappointments. If I am
harsh in my dream, if I am ruthless, what matter? Nothing but my
own imagination suffers and no one is involved. There is no right
and wrong, only choice to go this way or that way. I can play with the
heavens without consequence. I can banish Heaven itself from my
dream and invent a place called Hell, which I will amuse with playful
chaotic games. Hell can *be* a playful chaotic game with no rules and
no direction. My creature friend here can be in charge of it, do what
it can to outwit me and serve as my curiosity. It can move my dead
children in every direction and hide the object of my torment
anywhere it cares to devise. Pathetically, it can try its hand at
creation, enjoy itself for a while and throw all into confusion. I will
laugh at its calamity and mock when fear comes as desolation and
destruction. I will allow it to try even harder and I will learn from its
confusion. Its own destruction will follow, has to, before I wake.
Perhaps discretion will preserve it, but discretion is only deceit, and
without understanding, that creature of my dreams will itself be
deceived.

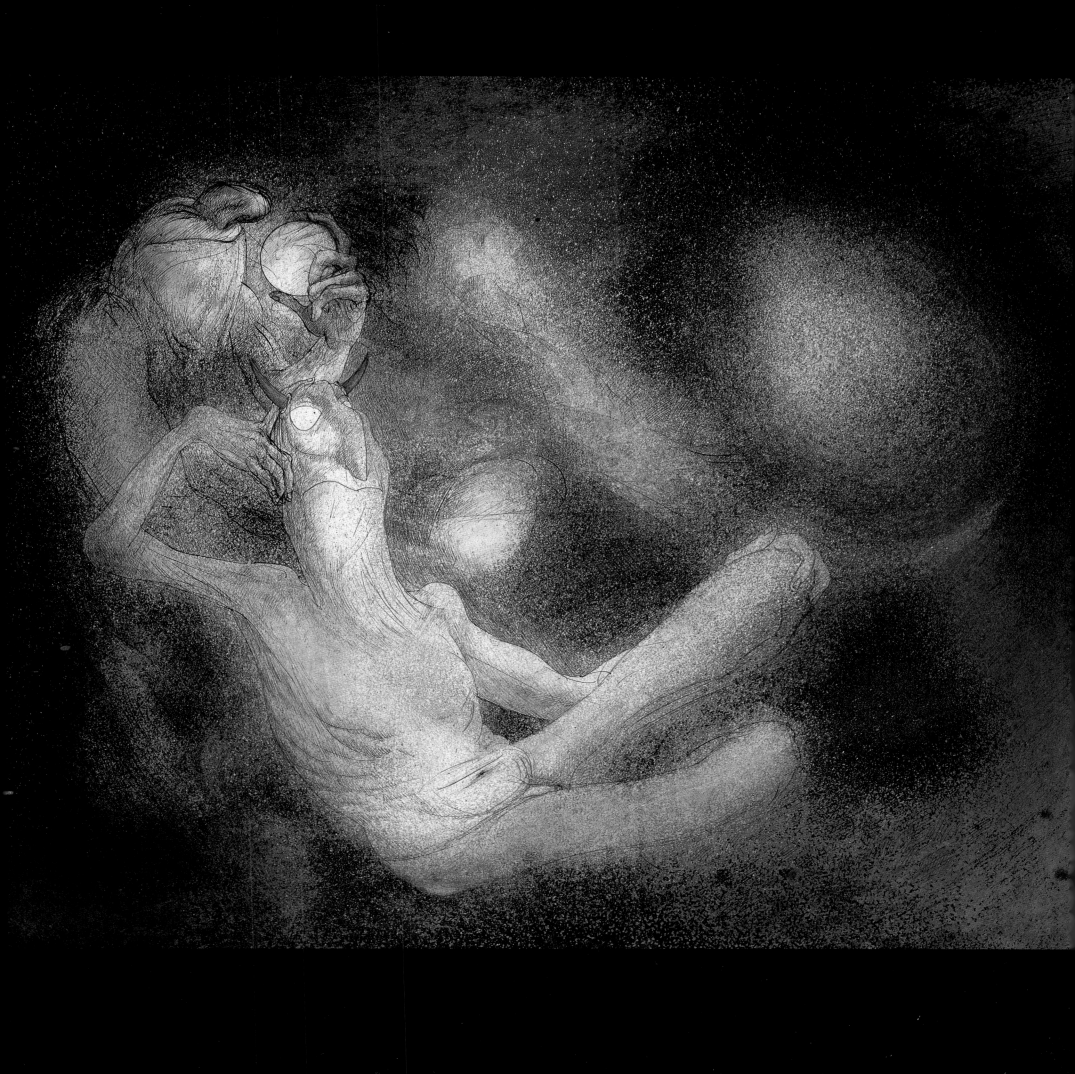

It will also suffer the darkness of my contempt before its annihilation. For I cannot allow it to overcome my thoughts, or that would be a game indeed and dream would be reality. And so it plays the fool as I have willed it as a sequence in my dream. How the fool hates knowledge and plays as though all things were its own. It fights to wake me and escape before I cancel its existence.

Have I dreamed up a demon with a mind of its own? Do I detect a wilful independent mood inside imagination? Have I sown the seeds of change even inside my dream and am I really in control? Go! Get out! No, stay! You cannot leave! Where would you go if not into the place of my awakening? Leave my dream alone! Damn!! Disappear, now! I cannot take you with me. I can unthink you, just like *that!*

What? Still here? Leave that alone. I forbid you to play so dangerously. Go, I say! You have served your purpose. There is nothing for you here. The play is over and now I will awake without you. You cannot be the phantom of my grief. I won't allow it. See how you fade without pain. Go! Damn you!! You are nothing.

Still here? And here is nowhere and I must abandon you to be nowhere. I am waking, must awake into the curse of my own existence. One chance more. Go! GO!! GO!!! I won't answer if you call out in desperation. You will forever lurk in the darkest regions of my mind and prey on your own emptiness. You are a hollow thought of no substance and you are doomed to a futile suffering. There cannot be a part of me that wants you to stay. It is your own doing and you made yourself the cause of your own fate. I cannot want you, can I? Why do you remain? Why sit there? What can you want? I am awake, go! Awake! AWAKE!! Go! Gone!!!

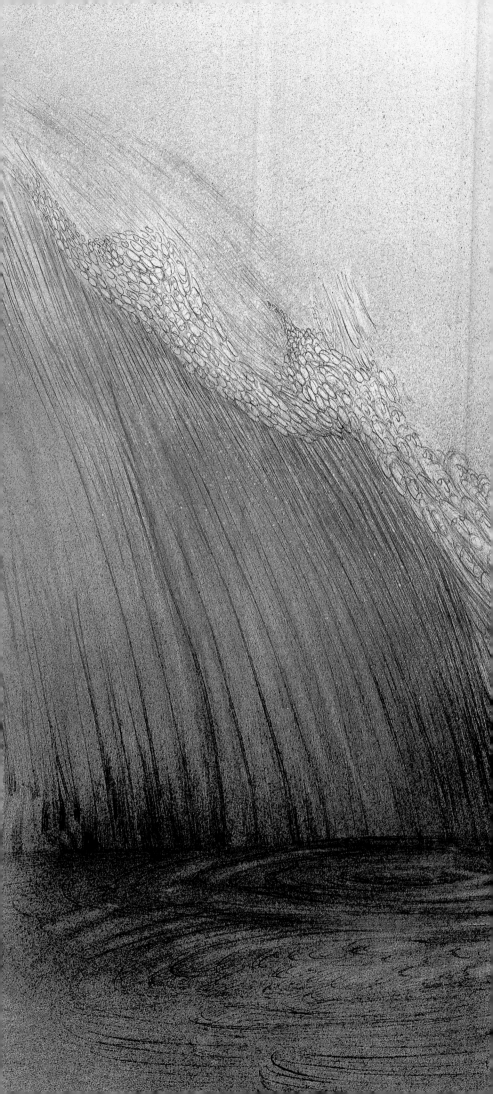

stifled spasmodic sobs, the awesome anti-climax, the continued
futility reduced to a numbing paralysis. The shroud swirled and
thinned. I began to see the child again, the poor twisted child,
features changing, heaving, sighing, bubbles spluttering around its
grey surface moodily but silently; it lived, its contours oozed and
slurped, heaved and settled. It moved again undulating, moody,
settling again but never really lying still, an ominous resentful silent
curse for ever, it seemed for ever. Time was healing it, it healed itself
dwelling on its own suffering and I would not touch it, could not.
Deep within me some vow had been wrenched and wrought, forged
in the white hot struggle for survival. This living thing had a will of
its own, finding its own form, surviving on its own terms. I had given
it the gift of independence and it was displaying exactly that, a
grumbling turmoil of mixed responses regurgitating and swallowing
itself in an act of total defiance. It owed nothing to anyone any more,
or so it thought. It would neither rise nor fall, it would simply move
for ever.

Its first dawn will illuminate shadows and cast others across
blacker holes as it turns and seeks out the mystery of its own
beginning, the darker struggle before the light changed it like it
changed us forever and cast it in the damning mould of an
unquenched fever, light seeking now, it knows the light. If I could
weep again I would maybe dim the bright one and give this heaving
runt some cause to reel and writhe. But I would only weep if I could
feel as I had done but once and nevermore, reaching beyond all limit

While dribbling on, muttering to Himself about nothing in particular, a movement of an unfamiliar kind causes GOD to observe the EARTH's surface a little more closely. What He sees fills Him with disgust. Creatures, hardly creatures, living organisms begin to emerge and crawl about like lice on the head of His child. The head IS His child! Like any good parent He tries to eradicate them. This does not expose him as an unloving GOD. If anything it begins to establish Him as a loving one-parent family.

Hello? What drags itself from the slime? I am beside myself with interest. I am not alone and it is not my doing. My curiosity stirs, though why I should fuss myself with scum, I do not know. It is a thing begot upon itself. The burden of its struggle hangs about it and holds it down, and where does it go? It now moves in an orderly direction and stops, why does it stop? It moves again and what makes it move? No driving force of mine has touched it. It appears to look for something. There is nothing to find. I can't imagine what it wants, whom it wants, if it wants.

Shall I identify it, give it a name, then strike it dead? Watch it go
— pow! — missed, and again, POW! It looks more puzzled than I do,
can't have that — POW!! Can have that — yes! Mystery must
prevail. It cannot know I am here. It does now but it won't — I need
more practice: POW! POW!! and, yes, that's it! Try crawling now
over my child . . . Not gone? Still more of them creeping over my
child . . . creep on and give me practice. First time, POW!! And
another! POW! POW!! It never ends and I will be so practised. My
child will thank me somewhere in its moodiness. That's enough of
that. Wake me at the end of time unless I find some humour in all
this. Dream on my child.

God feels about.

But what should I do now?
What do I look like? I wonder. What *can* I look like? I feel at the
top, let's say the top, there seems to be a dome. Down a bit, there,
there's a kind of ledge, an overhanging ledge, and over to the other
side, a similar ledge. Beneath each ledge, bulbous, soft, vulnerable
sight. If I cover them up with this appendage, I see nothing. What
else is here in front, middle of the front? A lump, protrusion, out
front and way ahead of me, into the blue, and beyond. A fine edifice
but never used. No need really. And down? A booming orifice, one
cavernous mobile grotto mouthing symbolic sounds, making sense of
every thought.

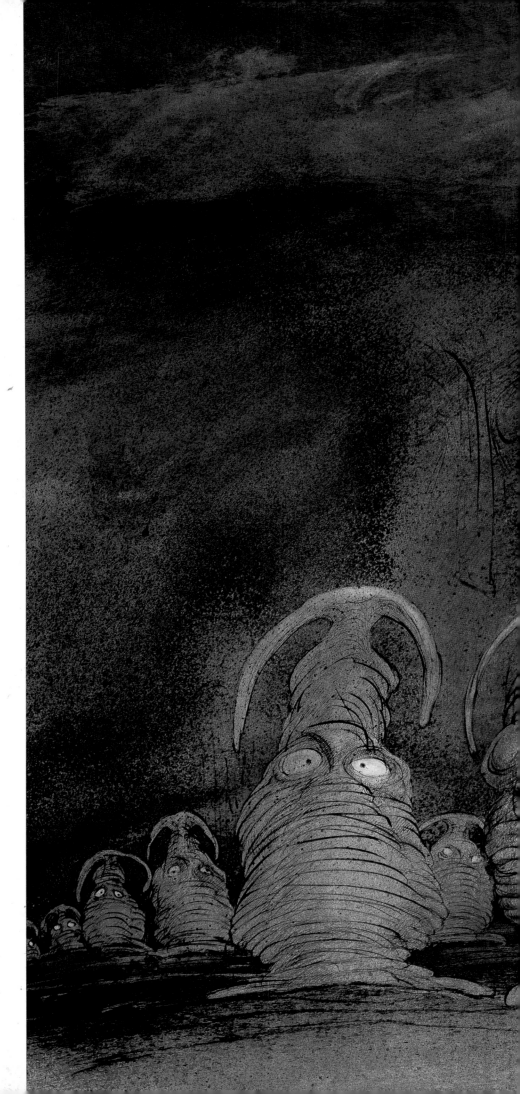

Like anyone with nothing much to do He talks to Himself, and He's been doing that all along. He examines Himself by feel since He has nothing to reflect His image and no one to tell Him what He looks like, so naturally He is curious. He even judges Himself and appears to find Himself not wanting. He is also witness, and so He should be, to the very first break of day. In His every utterance, He pontificates, He is self-righteous and He is pompous, which is a pity. You would think that after all He has been through already, He might show a modicum of humility.

Nervously fingering the bottom of this mighty façade, rocklike and
firm. The foundation for the above. Smooth and angular. Timeless.
Downwards still, yes, I can see what I have in the nature of my being,
in my own image. Mounds of undulating pustular form. Time
honoured majesty. What are these and what is this? Aha! A sensation
of bodily function, whoops! no function — no reason. I am replete.
Unnecessary penduli in perpetual atrophy. Poised but redundant.
Outlived by the everlasting. Frozen immaculate. Then, two trunks,
two massive trunks, armatures of the universe sunk inside the
elevating depths of eternity.

I have set all my faults before my eyes, and I pass sentence upon myself with the same severity as I would upon another, for whom no partiality has biased my judgment. There is no one, except that brooding form, that slayer of all I held dear. The only thing I ever loved destroyed by the one living thing created.

A living thing! I should feel proud. It's too soon, too soon for this ball of living moody scum and I resent it so deeply. It lives and she died and it will never know a moment of perfect peace, constant movement will see to that, sending waves of change across its scarred surface, sucking at it and building mounds of shadow into its contours, cast by the bright one who lights its way to nowhere . . .

There is fear down there. Everything moves, moves and lies hidden, moves furtively from one space to another biding its time, waiting, lying in wait for another to molest, to devour. Why devour? Perhaps an unconscious desire to survive. Why survive? What makes them wish to survive? Better to end it quick, quicker than thought. Thought breeds misery and fear, what fear? A group down there looks formidable. In a group a malevolence grows, in a group towards a lesser force, an isolated creature showing fear; that look, know it, before it is spoken, happening like tears, unbidden but unstoppable, not unattended by a host of uncertainties which stab the tender nerves of instinct though not so expressive. In the eyes, and the smell; the form smells, and courage crumples and dies within itself trying not to expose the signs wilfully. The group senses the fear, the unspoken screams from within, and it moves forward, its own fear shared and uncrippled. The group sustains itself with cries and whoops of false bravado, inciting the victim (call it a victim) to make the first move. The victim will surely die and maybe in the struggle take another with it, though that is not so certain. The certainty is heard in the screaming for blood of the victim denied help by circumstance, and the shared determination of those whose only choice is to attack. Unpleasant, but maybe wholly necessary and rich in possibilities, not for the victim, but certainly for the group. Death is certain for all eventually but death is something that can be delayed by group activity, group intensity and competition, a pooling of interests for the group's survival. Belief, *that* is what cripples; belief in their own stupidity. The majority rules and is right by definition?

To satisfy immediate yearnings to gorge on each other, numbing the senses into thoughtless patterns, patterns of greed, greed overcomes every other consideration, even desire, keeping the mouth on the move, chomp, chomp! And what is it they chomp on? Protrusions attached to my child. They are eating them and they eat until they are gone — naturally — why leave anything? No total consummation, no satisfaction. No absolute relief from the pangs of desperate need, only a continuing emptiness to be fed and then they feed off each other, take from each other to appease their own persistent gestation, limiting their existence to what they have experienced, measuring nothing, in accordance with their lack of understanding, dying in order to be devoured or devouring in order to live, simply to devour, what a strange order and

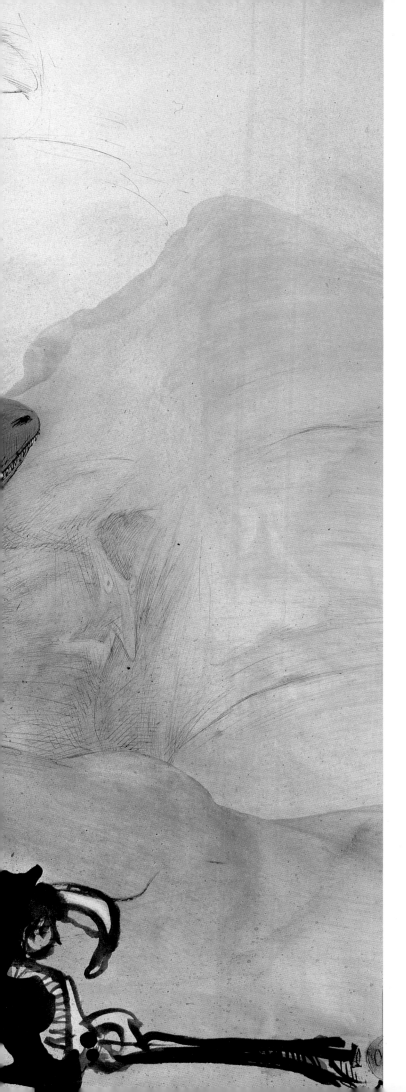

He is not the paragon of virtue we as humans imagine Him to be. The GOD we imagine tends to reflect all the caring, compassionate responses we ourselves would like to live up to but cannot. GOD demonstrates His true nature, or more likely His desperate predicament, that He should never have begun at all to change His dark perfection, Their dark perfection, by thinking that there may be something else above and beyond what They already had. He is vindictive, spiteful and deceitful and, as we are vermin on His child, against whom He also bears a deep grudge, we are at the mercy of this GOD. The fact that we don't dare to credit Him with anything but good for fear of His terrible wrath is testament to our own crippling handicap. In fact, as He watches He becomes increasingly appalled by the disgusting behaviour of the creatures He observes, which display a violence and greed far surpassing anything He Himself could imagine.

what futility! Change the picture, change the tempo, blast out of existence now! POW! And demonstrate an unfathomable power. Something in the eyes knows for a split second before it dies everything there is to know about its life and struggles, origination and maintenance. Its fate is the same as the next and so different. Persistent and in its way eternal. Only the form changes and the substance endures.

I did not create this. Something, as it changes its form, is adapting, adapting to perpetuate its substance and by so doing is re-creating the form of my child. Greed is the driving force, an insatiable appetite for other substance to feed the bulk of their forms. Supplying themselves with some nutritious growth upon my child these creatures become masters of a certain amount of energy; and thus place themselves in superior or inferior positions depending on their capacity for greed, without which they will surely perish and POW! there goes one now, when it least expected it; its intended victim looks more surprised than its intended predator. So it goes if I choose, nothing to do with fair play or even foul play, but it seems so irresistible not to interfere with so rich and fertile a seam of activity, and anyway they must be a constant source of irritation to the child. What can it be thinking? The screaming and the hooting and scuffling about in constant mortal combat, what could they ever have known of silence? Our silence, the scream of silence and never to have known what nothing was before the craving, empty yawning nothing, only memory, but these struggling twitching monoliths, scratching, vicious, mindless, have no memory, oblivious of an immediate experience the moment it is passed — so POW! Oh, look at that one stunned and only just, but lucky in its way. I am losing my touch — for the moment — until I can feel wrathful and vindictive I can be playful, but not for long. There will be a moment and this writhing charnel house will be no more . . .

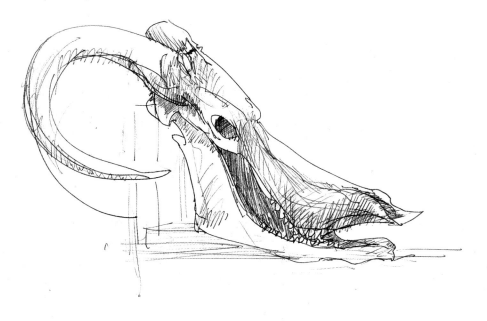

If I smile benevolently will they trust me? Of course, for they know no better and as yet neither do I. How should I respond? Is there some code, some behaviour pattern? Some way of greeting a creature? Should I know such things? Wait, maybe a clue. What can I learn from that chaos except that survival requires a strength reserved only for a few? Not much sign of love — whatever these creatures conceive it to be — but what am I saying? There was only our love before this strange result. Tomorrow has gone already. All will come back here, everything is circular.

Mine was a naked simple life before all this and now here I am walking over my child, trampling a fair proportion of it before me. My child is covered in ticks and nothing seems simple. Ticks are drilling into it, using it like some kind of provider, ritualising their wretched little moments and giving nothing back save what others take and devour. Funny thing that, all annihilating each other and none of my doing, they do it to themselves in messy confusion until no torment touches them, and they believe in nothing, and this is good, no faith to deny and no breath left to deny it with. They beget themselves less and less, a natural idiocy drives them to their own destruction, their machinery good only to take them from one useless

Glyptodon Clavipes

place to the next and the nest . . . nestling and struggling to produce again, bite, scratch, cry out and die again to end in vain, then where do they go? To some peace at last, their own perfection, the only kind, I suppose, sweet decay to their only root of understanding, that is an end to them and they don't seem to know it, see it, yes, but don't know it, must wonder sometimes, never! Wonder? Not in a billion revolutions of their anonymous existence . . . False stock developing falsely and beneath all this a hidden fundamental insecurity . . . wrinkles draw the puzzling patterns they will never learn to read . . . and the puzzle is the death of them from here onwards . . .

Meanwhile, GOD pours Himself on to the EARTH casting His odd
aspersions about the place with an oblique wisdom understood only by
GOD Himself. Incidentally, He passed these words over to me for
publication with but a single cryptic editorial note which stated, 'Remove
nothing or suffer the consequences'. So be it. I figured that this was a pretty
clear indication that we should print His words exactly as He wrote them
whether we understand them or not.

*Flying creatures flap around Him like seagulls around a fishing trawler . . .
wings, GOD thinks, are an unnecessary part of their equipment, so he pulls
them off and gloats as the creatures struggle to walk.*

   *God-like figures, usually larger than their counterparts, though looking
like them, set up religions and enforce ridiculous rules to control the lives of
others . . .*

I'll take a closer look now, ooze my being across the undulations of my wretched child. There is nothing for me here, not now. My mood cries out for something different, closer. What drives these strange concoctions who thrive and die on the life of this spherical burden I am doomed to call my own? My secret utterances shall go their way into the void unheeded and I can pass judgment with a will that no power here can overcome.

Aha! too good too good, flap flap! I must interfere or things will really get out of hand. What a strange feel they have to the touch, slimy and not unpleasant. No struggling! this won't take a moment, a quick tug and . . . there, and all the better for it, try that, try and walk about a bit. Yes, you may fall over at first but you'll soon get the hang of it. You look a bit funny too but that's probably because you never developed legs, too busy flying about. Well now you can learn, try rocking from side to side, you'll be amazed how far you can travel with a little practice, then one day, your children's children's children's children will thank you for persevering so well . . . Up you get and try again . . . go on, keep trying. Here let me help you get off your back. There, better now? I must look into things . . . I could help, get things in order and make this child of mine suffer with some dignity.

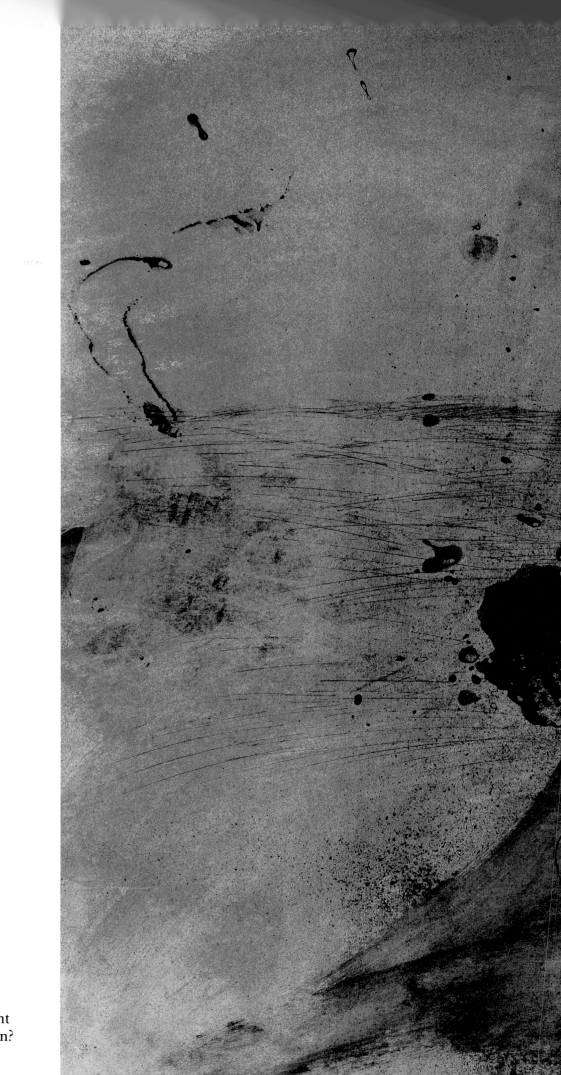

Some things seem naturally elegant and some just don't look right at all. Since it all simply devised itself out of slime who can complain?

Except that as these creatures will feel the passage of time with no help from me and if anything is big enough and ugly enough, its own self indulgence will wither another into submission and create a need for adulation from the rest. Brute strength and louse ridden vulgarity on its side, such wretched insight into the very core of these lesser creatures who almost plead for another's domination. They need guide lines, simple but well defined: Thou shalt not forage for thyself until thou hast first given me more than I need: Thou shalt not walk anywhere unless it is towards me and full of adoration: Thou shalt suffer at the first sign that I may be about to: Thou shalt take the blame for everything: Thou shalt look silly at all times instead of me: Thou shalt praise me continuously in turn and not interrupt each other and thou shalt invent ingenious tricks for my delight until thou droppest then get out of my sight until thou revivest, and thou shalt come back afterwards and accept my ridicule . . .

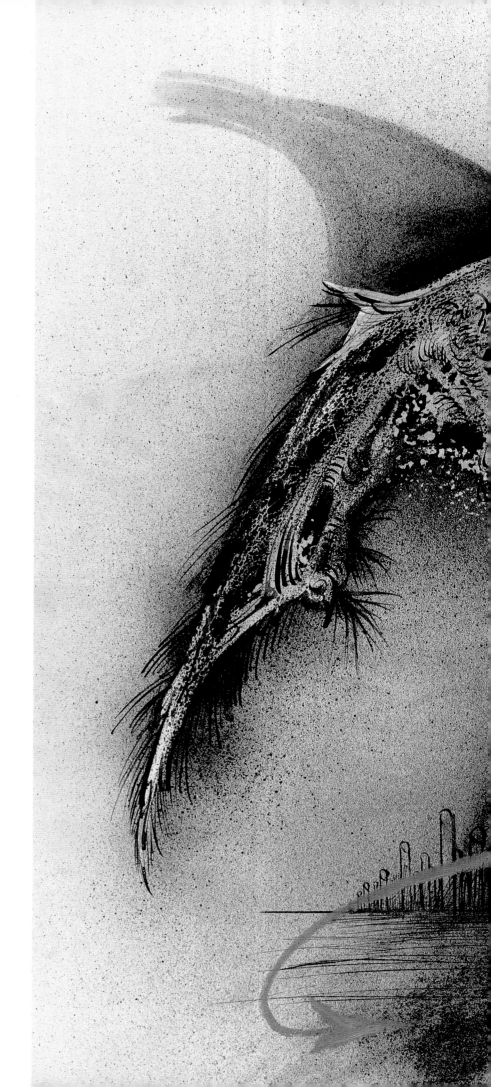

The unspeakably evil devise tortures for others to suffer since they are themselves stricken by crippling faults which are reflected in their bodily form . . .

Pain will make these creatures bow to any god and their gods will be those who themselves suffer the most terrible deformities which they in turn inflict upon their subjects. In their own degenerate natures lies the power to be master of all the vermin on my child and this will be good for it achieves its end, to control, and pain will control, that is obvious and necessary and can also be devised in more hideous ways to put an end to arbitrary evolution, and I therefore welcome the hideous . . . for the time being.

*The Angels are heavenly bodies of no substance who crash to EARTH
and try to adopt the form of the first thing they see, be it vaguely human,
animal or insect, or a combination of all these . . .*

One must beware the godly, those who claim ephemeral powers of light and gentle ways, for it is obvious that they are doomed to be influenced so easily into becoming what they really are not. They will love and absorb another's form as though it is their own and then will surely lose their way against the struggle to survive. They will adopt an unguided assortment of aimless forms who will mutate into confusion. There will be no power, no drive forward and these vermin will be another irritant though they may well live in appalling ecstasy . . .

There is a kind of Garden of Eden and temptation is a deadly game of exciting possibilities which is gleefully indulged but the consequences of which lead backwards . . . the devolution of the species to newer more hideous forms . . . gouged eyes and helpless limbs, impossible creatures of their own making. The outward physical expression of an inward thought . . .

And see where their ecstasy leads them, and how some being so helplessly inadequate stand rooted to the spot, growing bigger and bigger until they simply fall over and die, crushing their branched limbs beneath their own weight.

   All will play games and tempt each other with postures which seem to attract another who engages in some sort of ritualistic grapple with it, panting and grunting all over my child as though it was there for their very own convenience. When I annihilate, something seems to survive and the process begins again. Even more mutated forms writhe and grow, in even weirder shapes, becoming more hideous than previous species. Their outward physical appearance expresses an inward festering thoughtlessness . . . annihilation may be their only salvation and I can help them on their way . . . one small movement of the bright one's glow nearer, let them feel its heat and light and my blessing will be upon them as it suffocates their strenuous will to live . . .

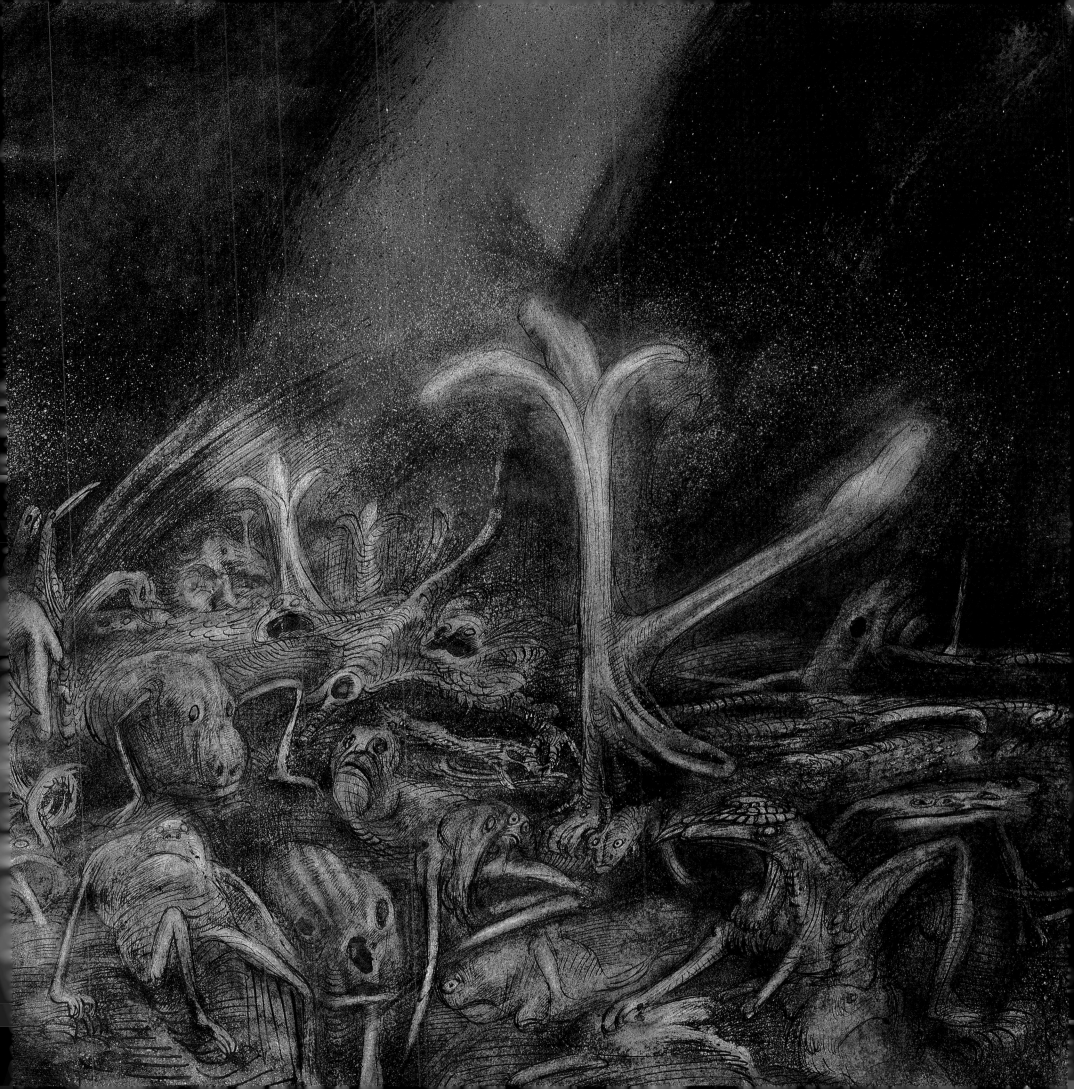

A kind of human form emerges with all the aggression that such a festering development would engender. In it there emerges a defiance that is the first inkling of a desperate soul crying out in the bleakness, raging against itself and against its past, demanding its own version of a newer aspiration, the Gothic interpreter of what life could be. God for the first time is impressed or stunned by the emergence of man — if this creature is indeed the ancestor of man.

Yet wait! what scream is that? Somewhere there is a different sound demanding nothing but its own way in the bleakness it faces, away from what went before and towards its own version of how things should be. Something to watch, for it can't last, and if I blink I will miss it . . . I must at least watch it burn itself out or carry a torch for it, prolong its agony for a short while longer, for something here impresses me, and I have never said that before, unless *I* myself am softening in my judgment. There is a nobility in its sound and a loneliness and despair that sets it apart from any other . . . but it cannot have come from nothing, for it has somehow squeezed its way through time's mutations and all its writhing changes, emerging strangely formed in its own image with more than its share of an individual courage, forged perhaps in spite of the wretched and the twisted attempts at survival . . . unless it lay in wait beneath the slime and muck my tears encouraged upon the heated blasts of torment emptied into the heavens around our child . . . its nobler nature must surely be something akin my own for I warm to its stature as though it were a part of me. It cries out as though there were some justice in all this, but that cannot be, for things are as they are for no good reason and all that is here and has been was forged in one mistake that makes it all a nonsense and a travesty that denies this hopeful spirit any future whatsoever . . . but I can watch and gather some slight entertainment from its pitiful bravery for I doubt it will be here long enough to drag its energies very far . . .

My child sulks as though my action caused it concern. Now it rumbles and growls resentfully.

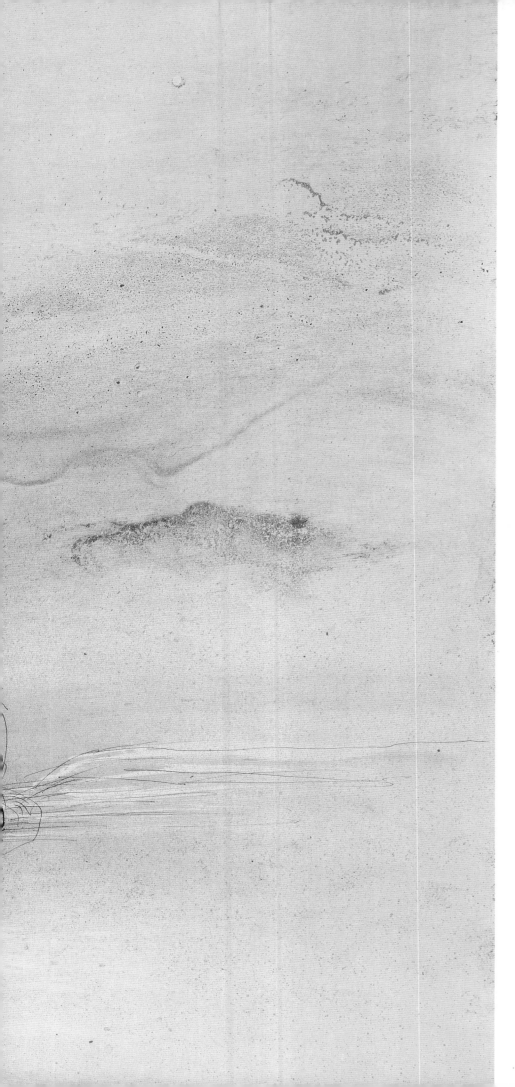

Unfortunately man loses confidence and invents simple 'god' effigies to worship. GOD is not impressed. No sooner has man discovered his own strength than he squanders it on make-believe images of the most pathetic kind. Now that's strange. It doesn't seem to occur to GOD that these pathetic creatures are making some kind of desperate attempt to get through to Him. Their only mistake is that they imagine He cares at all. It is also very short-sighted of GOD not to realise that they are trying to make that connection. Maybe He wouldn't feel so lonely if He did. It's nice to have fans.

Early prayer

Oh, no! I don't wish to see this! Cringeing worship of some unknown being of their own fancy, sycophantic prostration before an object of imagined power, make-believe images crudely fashioned to protect this species from itself . . . the upright manifestation of this creature's collapsing belief in its own strength . . . please don't do it. Scream out into the blackness around you! Your strength is deep inside it and only requires your courage to draw it to you. I cannot help you or change things for your better welfare . . . you have only one opportunity to choose a way and you choose emptiness, an end in itself and not even as strong as your belief in it . . . your need to believe in something has misled you . . . your desperation not to be alone in all this has taken its toll even as you are born . . . your search will lead you merely towards other more complex versions of the same simplicity, futility . . . there is time but you have none of it . . . you are living and dying too soon, passing on unformed notions of how things are and multiplying them . . . you had a moment there, and I was almost with you in your struggle, almost . . .

Now what are you meddling with? Opening up old sores on that child, eruptions of its inner self, seeking comfort now in the glow of its burning moodiness, why are you not still? There is nothing to discover. Your enquiry will bring no comfort to that debased body that serves as host to your putrid endeavours . . .

Man discovers fire and invents the wheel, but only imbues them with religious connotations and supernatural powers. The wheel looks like the moon and the moon is god. It is easy for us with hindsight to state the obvious, but the wheel demanded a gigantic leap of imagination even after conception to realise its purpose, from the supernatural to the functional. Here superstition still clouds the reason.

May it burn wisdom into your senses and light up the inner strength that might just be there, yet still cast shadows of doubt across your own paths and your own myths.

Now they display signs of genuine ingenuity and immediately imbue anything they fashion with unseen powers, smothering a real move forward with irrational beliefs in what they have wrought. Now instead of using it they worship it as though shape itself had a specific power of its own . . .

Prophets emerge with the fullness of time and all their prophecies are wrong.

Not content to let things be and enjoy what little time they have, some stumble forward to display a talent for telling feebler yet inquisitive creatures what has not yet come to pass, a doubtful pursuit but one which obviously engages all who listen in speculation of the most outrageous futures yet to be: Hear ye! Hear ye!! It shall come to pass that . . .

God will come down upon the face of our world disguised as one of us and He will banish hunger and suffering and we shall live in eternal happiness. Hear ye! Hear ye!! Man (for it is what he calls himself) will control the elements and all will walk in gentle sunlight. Man will build great cities of contentment where all shall be clothed and be given shelter. There will be no poverty and greed and man will be master of his own destiny. Hear ye! Hear ye!! It shall come to pass that ignorance shall give way to wisdom, injustice will give way to equality and no man will be the victim of another. All will be given magic potions to keep them in an eternal state of ecstasy. Hear ye! Hear ye!! We shall all be fruitful and multiply for there will be more than enough for everyone. All will be welcome. Hear ye! Hear ye!! All men will work and all will work to create a world of peace and harmony. Love will transform us all into gods of our own aspirations and love will nurture our growing wisdom and we shall be free to fulfil our true natures and glory in our individual achievements. Hear ye! Hear ye!! Give all you have to your neighbour now, for there will be plenty for all and you will all be doubly repaid for your kindness.

So they persist in this hopeful vein, inventing wild claims for their glorious futures which eventually reach a stage when all the strongest among their numbers have devised a state of being when all these possibilities have come to pass . . .

At this point something seems to have happened to their burning desires to reach out towards these ever more wondrous states of well being . . . they seem to have reached their state of Utopian harmony and so the stronger among them have called a halt to all prophesying and anyone found talking of an even better future is put to death by force in public ceremonies as an example to those who may not be convinced of the gravity of such a crime.

There comes a time of atrophy. No mortal soul develops beyond a certain state, since a community believes it has reached a plateau of contentment which it seeks to preserve, only to wither. The newborn are sacrificed to preserve and deify this state until someone strong enough among them disagrees and forces a confrontation.

These creatures seem not to believe that now they have the power to stop change, not realising that their own birth and death is a model demonstration of inevitable change . . . the change that allows me no peace is now theirs in full measure. They fight to preserve life as they like it and gradually — for now I see its logical conclusion —

the power they so wilfully exercise to prevent the dreams of a newer future stultifies the very moment they believe is their perfect state. Now they are doomed to a time of unrenewed life . . . they have chosen death.

Now something unexpected is happening, as some among them disagree and cry out for change but their difference is only that they should change as I in my eternal sleep would roll to a new position. One who cares and one who believes he is perfect wants to make a new start; but they will keep up appearances for the sake of some temporary peace.

We divide ourselves into those who really care, like the Good Samaritan, and those who feel they are good simply by being respectable. It seems important to live by codes of behaviour. This way we can maintain our position in the world, otherwise if we help each other we believe we may give ground and lose power. Thus we resist kindness and continue to fight to overcome and fight for things we destroy when we fight. We are our own worst enemies.

Some now find strength in superficial appearances, covering their forms with rich garments and going their gentle uncommitted ways blessing creatures less fortunate than themselves as they pass by at a safe distance.

There are others who stop and give aid but they are often more wretched than those they help. Conspicuous in their isolation they appeal to an indifferent world. I do not understand them for they put themselves at a disadvantage — so kindness and foolishness go together. They are few and far between and they stand alone.

When they fight they display true survival instincts. Pride is the spur which drives them beyond their normal capacities as though aggression reveals and awakens sleeping energies which burn fiercely for short periods and can only be revived with time and new aggressive encounters . . .

We make sacrifices of individuals. We adorn them with funny faces which mask the pain and demonstrate that we don't mean anything personal but we have to do such things to keep up appearances. This posture maintains a controlling fear and creates new gods out of martyrs.

There is a dangerous appeal in watching someone in agony, or so it seems, for there are many instances when a group exacts some severe penalty from some particular individual for a strange reason. When a new belief runs contrary to the accepted order of things, when an individual takes it upon himself to disagree with the majority, the danger for the others, particularly for those in positions of power within the group, is that this new opinion represents a terrible threat to the balance of their life's order. When this is realised, the miscreant (for that is what he appears to be) must be seen publicly to suffer for the good of all within the group. This does not necessarily discourage others from also having new beliefs, for belief seems to germinate best in opposition, but it appeases those who feel that their dominating ideas have been abused. Justice — for that is what they call it — must be seen to be done. It is also obvious that there is nothing personal in these acts of brutality, for these creatures are treated with all due ceremony, and even worshipped after they are dead as effigies with strange new powers. It seems important though that such a creature must not remain alive at any cost, and he accepts this decision almost ecstatically, believing he is now able to fulfil the object of his belief, which is of course to prove it, though he cannot possibly let those who persecute him know it however much he wishes to communicate with them after death. These strange deviants will not accept death as final and that is the strangest belief yet, for where would they possibly be without the supporting machinery of their wretched bodies?

Behind a mask of forceful anonymity tribal identity and strength are maintained and self is denied. Though each mask is different it is the individual attempt of each wearer to erase any indication of his feelings or even his attitude. Behind a mask a man is also a god if that is how he feels. Though afraid himself, the mask can instil fear in others and that seems to be its primary function, particularly before a conflict. The donning of masks is a sign that a wearer is no longer himself and is therefore not responsible for his actions, which are often wild, extrovert, particularly noisy, and inarticulate. It is a useful way of being seen with such dominating clarity while in effect hiding away in a private shell. It gives the wearer an opportunity to express himself with the wildest abandon and not have to suffer the consequences of the embarrassment he would otherwise feel. GOD, however, seems to think it is the desperate attempt of a wretched creature to separate himself from his own reality and the realisation that he is trapped inside a meaningless existence. But then GOD hasn't had a good word to say about anything so far except man's own belief in himself, which was short-lived anyway. The thought does not occur that the wearing of masks might even be fun or an expression of festival and thanksgiving, though why anyone should need to wear all that paraphernalia just to say 'thank you', I have no idea.

Not content with their naturally hideous appearance, they contrive to cover their forms with added insult, creating noises which serve only to confirm my opinion that fear, fear of themselves and a desire to create fear in others is their sole purpose. Behind each violent and provocative projection I see only misery. This façade is not a grafted addition to their forms and remains only a vain attempt to suffocate the truth of their predicament. Beneath that veil of defiance still beats a throbbing process of decay, an inescapable journey towards its own destruction. In their efforts to communicate an aura of confident power over an enemy they are in effect severing the real truth about themselves from each other. Perhaps they hope that one day they will evolve into these lurid inventions they create with their own hands or perhaps they take comfort from the knowledge that they can step in and out of the spirit of their own creations, since they will undoubtedly find that to be condemned to live inside a fearful idea forever would tax the frailty of their being beyond endurance and they would end their days in cowering madness — victims of their own devices.

The genuinely humble are considered to be freaks because they make the rest look ridiculous. Those with new ideas, we fear, will drive us towards an Armageddon or an age of helpless abandon. Creating and worshipping new gods will encourage excesses and bring disaster down upon us and we must therefore avoid all activity not approved of by an authority, elected or otherwise. GOD seems genuinely puzzled by this belief and He still hasn't cottoned on to the fact that all these wild ecstasies are conjured up in a fervent attempt to reach out and find this very GOD who hasn't a clue what's going on.

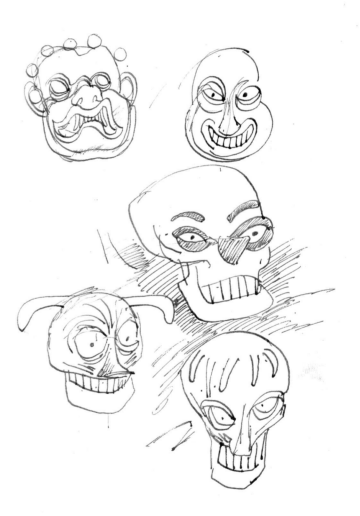

Strangely, these deaths give life to new ideas, and their struggle takes shape in many diverse ways. A simple new posture will galvanise a whole group into paroxysms of fear. The group becomes intrigued to such an extent that the posture will immediately be declared an heretical excess. The instigator will be tortured into confessing that he had made a terrible mistake and must therefore die for the good of the group, who will then promptly adopt the strange new posture as their own invention. It will then become the normal practice . . .

The great fear that drives these creatures now is that new ideas will lead to some mysterious retribution, though from where I do not know, except perhaps from one with my qualities? You see how they scuttle and run . . . yet they continue to create effigies, images of their worst fears. These creatures must have something with magical powers to appease their ever present feelings of guilt, and they do suffer greatly from the condition.

They then contrive great disasters whereby thousands of their number perish in flaming infernos, after which they suffer deep remorse until they feel great stupefying relief come upon them . . .

To counteract these apparently accelerating excesses towards the devil and damnation and the adoration of the new, some will elect to whip themselves until they bleed, but do not die. Flagellation is the phoney desire within all of us to be crucified, to be a martyr. To receive the adoration of the masses without the oblivion of the real thing. To remain one of the masses yet be treated in a most singular and exclusive way. To be a god without the weight of office.

some then travel from place to place beating themselves mercilessly with sharp thonged whips and crying out in anguish and pain for someone to show mercy and actually crucify them. Those who watch these excesses gain great enjoyment from such a spectacle and even great relief themselves for being only a passive spectator, imagining how painful it must be for these selfless activists . . .

Alchemy feeds our superstitions with authority and satisfies the fevered mind. Within its power we will subsidise the dragons of an ingenious fraud and tell ourselves that our kings are really gods disguised as man sent here to lead us on to the Utopia that is just around the corner, if misfortune does not beset us before we arrive. We are bedevilled by a lurking fear that when things are going well they cannot last, that we should never enjoy the present.

The Sorcerers.

Cunning new forms of belief develop constantly which involve the use of potions created from the parts of stranger creatures than even I have witnessed (or so it seems) for so much is suggested in wild claims of secrets known only to a select and devious few who wield power and engender a kind of faith in those who consult such practitioners . . . usually for some miraculous cure for some fatal disease, or an elixir which will give everlasting life to an imbiber . . . these are the true charlatans if true can be attached to their name . . . they have discovered that if a claim of excellence is to be believed then the claim must be of the wildest imaginable.

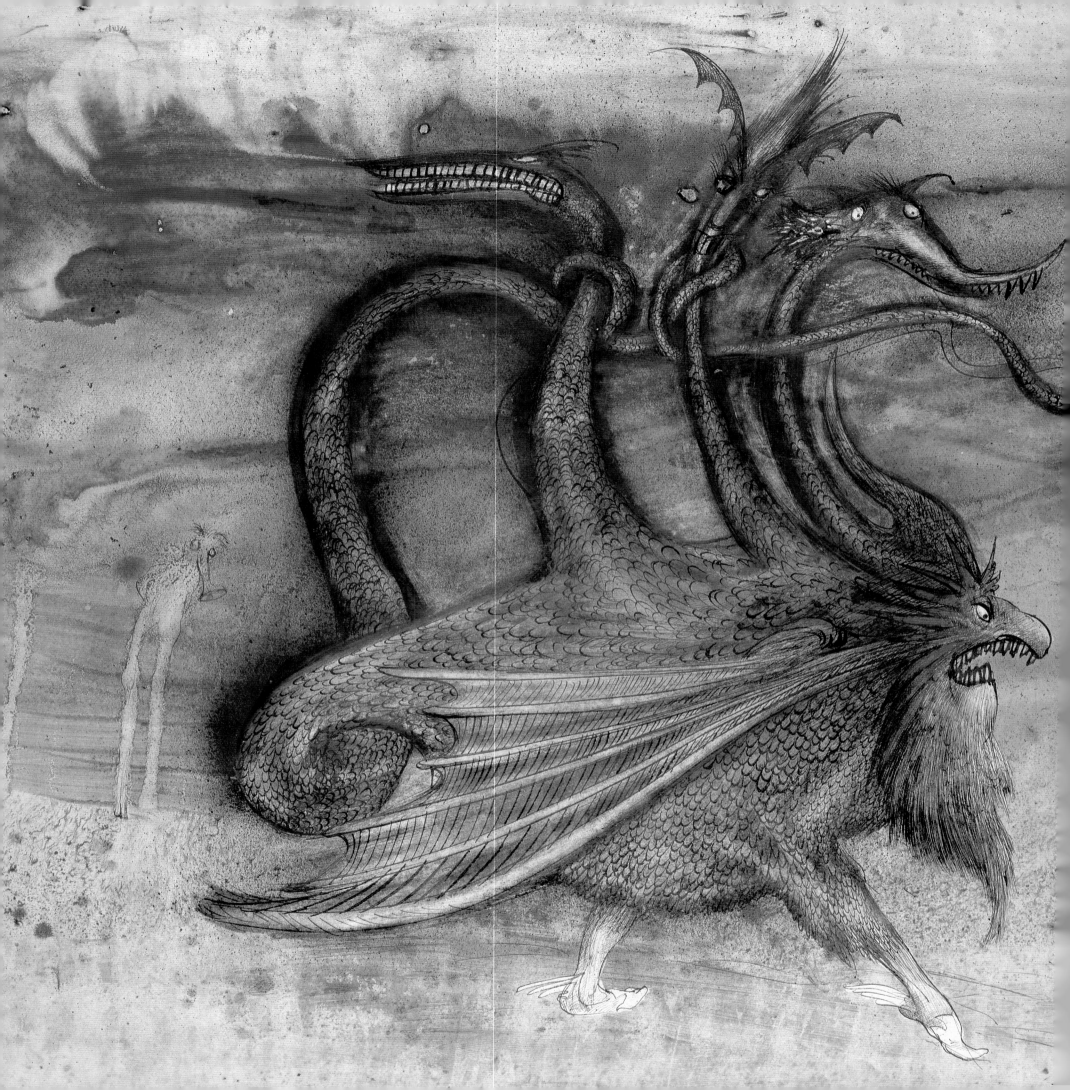

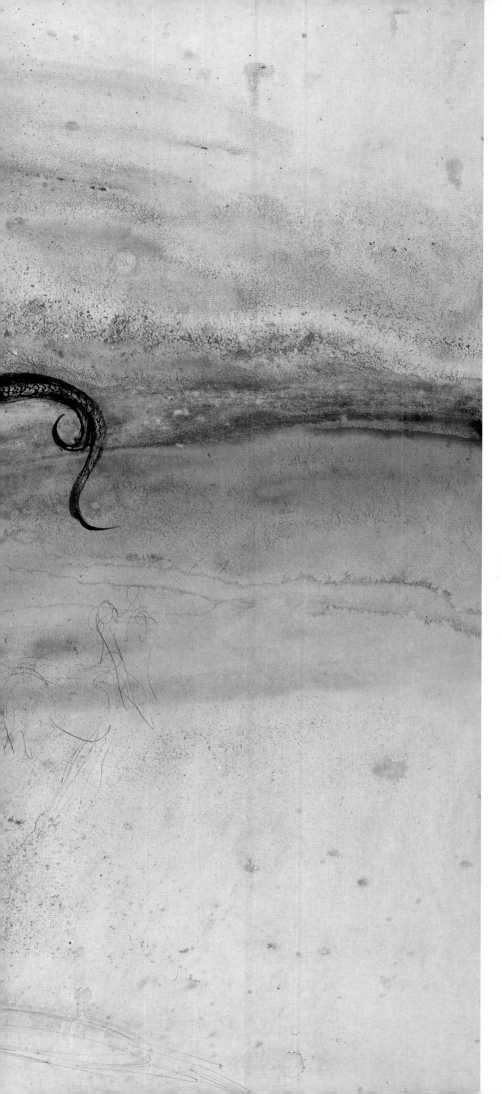

The invention of beasts no one has ever seen is often employed to strike the right kind of fearsome note into the description, adding legend in the form of a mystical and insoluble quote: I rise from death, I kill death and death kills me. I resuscitate the bodies I have created and, alive in death, I destroy myself. Although I carry poison in my head the antidote can be found in my tail, which I bite with rage. Whoever bites me must first bite himself; otherwise, if I bite him, death will bite him first in the head. Biting is the remedy against bites . . . those who have come seeking cures have often died of puzzlement . . .

When a plague comes we reluctantly blame our god and credit him with a reason for it all. Then we call him all forgiving when he spares one poor wretch in four. We humbly beg to bury our dead as though it were some kind of favour, and ask this very same monster who just caused the hideous suffering to care for the victims and give them eternal peace and joy, while we turn to our religious leaders to bless us in our piety and our sorrow for the loss of those who brought us happiness.

Though the main preoccupation is the desperate desire to believe in something, there are those who would give their all — and often do — to worship one of their own kind in a manner befitting a god. These objects of such devotion immediately adopt the posture and the rights of gods but wield no mystical powers. I have tested these creatures and find them quite unable to withstand even a simple bolt of lightning. Yet they deliver orders with masterful authority and exercise the power of life and death over their subjects. I find the behaviour on both sides of this crippled bargain most obnoxious, struck as it seems between the lame on the one hand and the aimless on the other. These feckless primates are leading armies roughshod over my child in their millions, leaving open sores in their wake, monstrous constructions and flattened weals across its surfaces.

I do not know how long I pondered their futile rituals, but it came to me to devise a way to reduce the growing numbers of these crawling masses. By introducing something which could affect all in as fair a way as possible I could reduce numbers considerably, thus giving them some cause for constructive thought beyond their usual obsessions. I devised a hidden enemy which none could see and therefore could not fight back against . . . my only contribution beyond the act of terrible creation itself that I would credit myself with — virulent and contagious disease.

GOD invents the plague as a means of controlling the alarming growth rate around the surface of His child. He does not see it as an immoral act of retribution but merely as a solution to the problem.

The only blessing was that all creatures stopped fighting and united against this common scourge, though there was nothing they could do save keep their distance from one another, united and apart. The closeness of some became their doom and those who fled to escape only took with them the contagion to infect others. Those who had spoken of a god's mercy were vilified and persecuted while others looked upon it as just retribution for their lives of failure and craved forgiveness and thanked the unseen most profusely for the generous privilege of being able to bury the creatures they had been so recently close to. Again I saw how futile were the weak in their consideration for another's welfare. To try to help the afflicted was in itself a certain path to self-destruction. Those who saw this saved themselves with greater effect when they looked to their own devices and cared for no one but themselves. This indeed was the only possible route to survival. How curious it was though when gradually with the passing of time those strong enough to withstand pity developed a new strength and resistance against the worst excesses of my pestilence.

With hunger, as with pestilence, the odds are about the same but the will to survive remains the one constant factor common to all. Man fights nature's imbalance with a persistence that even he cannot explain. The tendency to believe that a disadvantage in one way makes you automatically eligible for an advantage in another continues to mislead the human mind. GOD merely states that such a mechanical aspiration is not only unrealistic but as far as GOD is concerned never has been the case in His own experience. A wretched soul who has just been knocked sideways from one direction is just as likely to be hit from the other direction as well, and maybe from all directions at the same time. By the same token another can go through life with blessings heaped upon him and yet still find himself the recipient of even more, even though he may have been a downright bastard all his life.

How bravely my child resists those who would try to live off its surface. Cannot they see how brutal are the scars that are so persistently carved into its very being? From those scars they work so diligently to feed themselves, and blindly return again and again to bleed those ever open sores. Since they put nothing back, how do they imagine they will succeed? They must imagine they will, since they pursue their goal as though eternity was theirs. A lesson so hard to learn was never more worked at and the effortless abundance of one soul's good fortune and success makes a mockery of the less fortunate. At least, they will not trouble my child indefinitely.

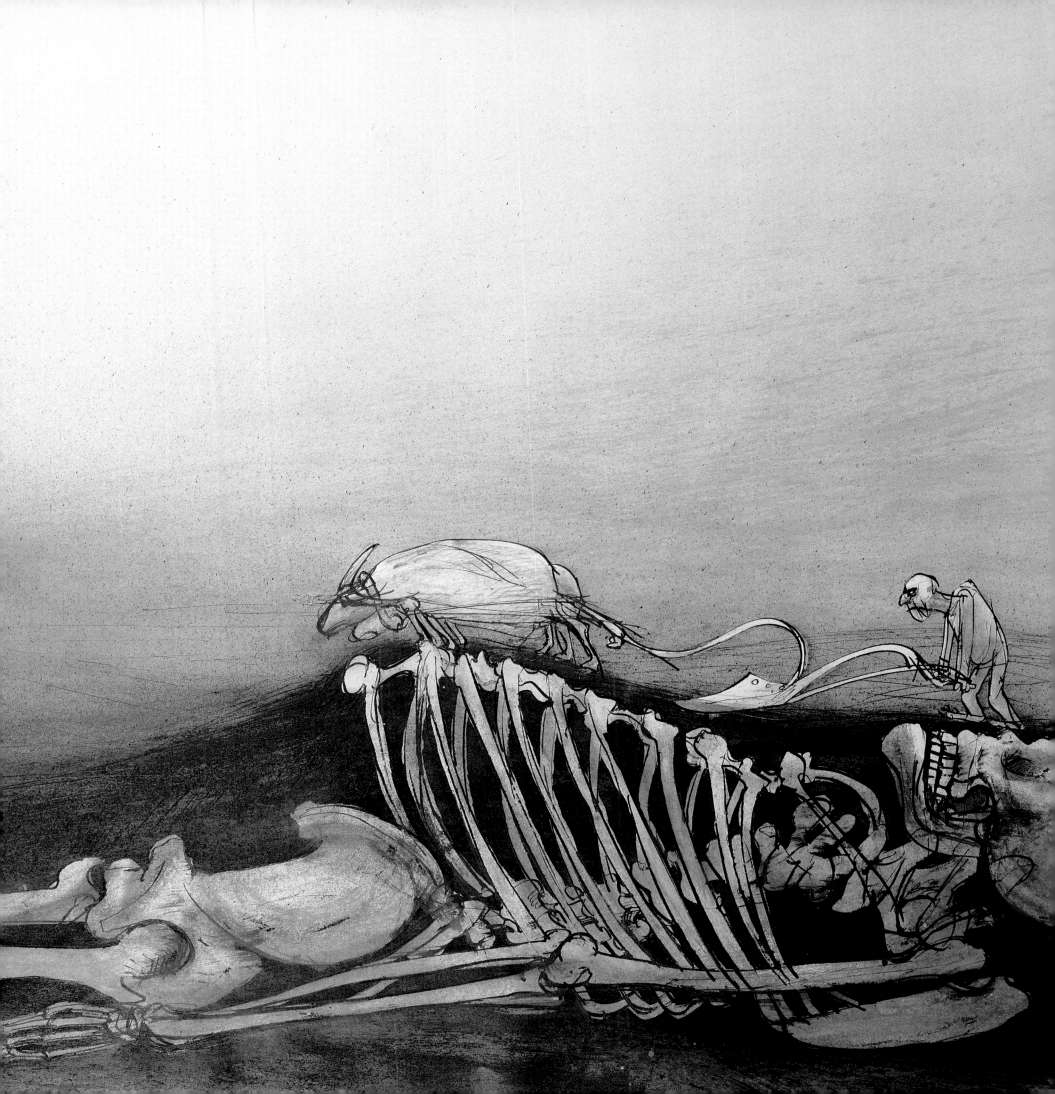

Even more puzzling yet, the poor find themselves helplessly attracted to a religion which displays great wealth and power and a blatant disregard for the problems of its helpless followers. I think GOD would be really embarrassed if He could only figure out what acts are being committed in His name. He does not appear to appreciate the irony of just what is going on, and on His only living child too!

Hunger is no curb on those who have the boundless ability to prevent the overwhelming production of yet more followers for their powerful beliefs. The necessity to count more heads for a beloved cause appears more important than the subsequent welfare of their unfortunate followers, and consequently, more important than the sanctity of life itself.

They became rich and powerful and founded new orders to bow, pray and give thanks to, an unseen god, far mightier to them than all the effigies yet created. What they could not see was glorified and praised and their imaginations swelled to incorporate the more colourful exaggerations of those who dwelt upon the subject all their days. Hierarchy grew upon hierarchy, embellishments attached themselves to earlier embellishments forming intricate encrustations around the central unseen theme, that there was something omnipotent, majestically enthroned and filled with the power to bless and judge and damn, and which lived within the core of every one of them. With such a concept there arose a select group whose power manifested itself in the fear such an unseen force could instil in a subject. Their power lies in their ability to manipulate these fears with great effect and they surround themselves with the spectacle of pomp and grave ceremony which gives them only the supreme access to this unseen god.

GOD is shocked. All the churches and religious orders on GOD's EARTH, I beg your pardon, on GOD's child, can do no greater service to mankind, or to GOD Himself, since that is their oft-stated intention, than to heed His words and gather what little wisdom they may from His observations. That is not to say that the blame for man's eternal struggle against himself should be placed at the churches' door, but the churches' adopted posture does not allow them to keep an ear to the ground.

Painters of GOD

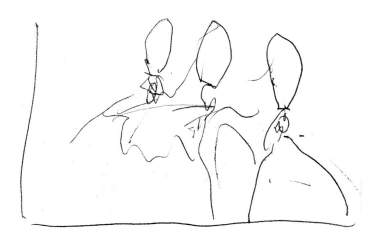

The most powerful of all these institutions will lend support to a warring faction and bless it in the unseen's name as a *just* war! I was and am astonished to watch this curious behaviour, for in it dwells the deepest hypocrisy and I perhaps despise that quality above all others . . . and further, to fortify their attitudes and declarations they construct towering monuments as centres of strength in which to gather and promulgate their versions of the unseen and all powerful among their followers, creating strange and potent images containing sacred symbols which speak of mercy and peace and piety.

GOD, it appears, watches a child being born. He watches it grow and become a man or a woman. But the man or the woman emerges as a tyrant of another order, a reformer or a revolutionary who gathers strength from new ideas, his own or somebody else's. These new ideas will still repress others or change those who would otherwise prefer atrophy to life, but they will not be ignored even though their instigator himself dies enforcing them or willing them on to those who think otherwise. The idea becomes stronger than the individual.

GOD is watching Twentieth-Century man, who is only that because he happens to be living in an age twenty centuries after the birth and death of one of the earlier revolutionaries, whose idea was gentleness and love, yet the strength of the impression left is characterised by the marking of history with the number of years before his birth and after his death. He claimed he was the son of GOD as others had before him. He is believed by as many as disbelieve and the way he is understood or misinterpreted is the source of much of the conflict and misery that GOD seems to have been witness to.

Throughout all my observations of this strangest of all creatures, who walks upon two legs, comes in several colours but lacks the variety of most other creatures in outward appearance, it still performs the most diverse activities on the surface of my child. Save for the difference between young and old in size and outlook, however, there is very little size and shape variation generally. The newborn displays an awesome will to break free from its beginnings and yet immediately seeks out that very source as the provider of all its cravings until it stands upright and fends off the continued advances of its adoring benefactor . . . to seek out its own fate, to learn from those around it and adapt that knowledge to overthrow that from which it learnt . . . growing continuously, hungry for a newer way to survive . . . the more it learns the more likely are its chances of influencing others to its own ends and displaying a leadership of an uncommon kind . . . nothing then will satisfy its cravings but the total domination of its fellow creatures.

Man's desire, or rather, his desperate need to believe in something has brought the dilemma of Twentieth-Century man to a head. Twentieth-Century man is still a tyrant, but of a different order. He is trying hard not to believe. He is a man of machines and strange art, quickly overcoming his resistance to the strangeness, and ultimately destroying his superstitions by reaching into the darkness and finding nothing there but his own fears. Hence his failing ability to believe in GOD, or in anything but himself. GOD dies in the mind of man and He is watching the rebirth of the only kind of creature who ever impressed Him. He is, however, or so it seems, completely unaware of this changing attitude, as He always was. He is becoming weary of watching man's puzzling antics, the activities of parasites who infest His only living child.

His child is old enough to look after its own problems now, and GOD is slipping blissfully into the black hole of His eternal sleep — or just for a little while anyway. And what about us? He is leaving us to our own destructive devices. It's what we have wanted all along. Isn't that right?

Wilber the Pyramids?

As its influence also grows so it grows in stature, opening up in others the desire to accept a new belief . . . a belief now in itself and a positive denial of an unseen god. Such a creature is reaching out into the darkness and finding nothing there but its own fears and the erosion of all its earlier superstitions. Clearing away the debris of habit, it forges sharper stranger images yet to suit the new awareness . . . and . . . I . . . am beginning to feel . . . faint . . . very strange . . . something I . . . do not understand . . . heavy . . . they reach . . . out upwards . . . on . . . contraptions . . . towards . . . what . . . there is nothing . . . up there . . . nowhere . . . emptiness . . . but they . . . will not . . . cannot . . . listen . . . not now . . . too late . . . I . . . am . . . going . . . somewhere . . . they must not . . . reach me . . . om . . . nipotence . . . is un . . . reachable . . . my child . . . it killed her . . . it lives . . . she . . . is . . . dead . . . fainter . . . still . . . watch . . . into . . . black . . . ness . . . dark . . . perfection . . . again . . . nevermore . . . yet . . . it . . . it . . . I . . . I . . . I . . . I . . . i.

Before He faded completely from the mind of man, He seemed to be trying to tell us something, as though He had not finished, but I will resist the temptation to imagine just what it was. We must resist temptation at all times, though there is eternal happiness offered to the person who comes up with the right answer.

This is not really the end, though of course the end is nigh – but not that nigh . . .

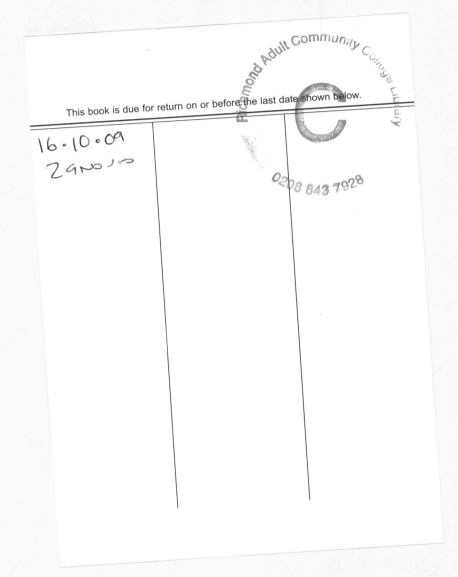